READY TO MAKE
MUSIC

IS THE
VIOLIN
FOR YOU?

ELAINE LANDAU

Lerner Publications Company · Minneapolis

Lerner Publications Company
A division of Lerner Publishing Group, Inc.
241 First Avenue North
Minneapolis, MN 55401 U.S.A.

Website address: www.lernerbooks.com

Library of Congress Cataloguing-in-Publication Data

Landau, Elaine.
        Is the violin for you? / by Elaine Landau.
            p.   cm. — (Ready to make music)
        Includes bibliographical references and index.
        ISBN: 978-0-7613-5423-9 (lib. bdg. : alk. paper)
            1. Violin—Instruction and study—Juvenile. I. Title.
        ML760.L26 2011
        787.2'19—dc22   2009045609

Manufactured in the United States of America
1 – DP – 7/15/10

CONTENTS

CHAPTER ONE

THE VIOLIN:
SOUND AND SONG THROUGH STRINGS

Picture this:

You walk out onstage. You're about to play a very difficult violin solo. Your palms are sweaty. You think you know how the passengers felt just before the *Titanic* went down. But as you lift your bow to play, everything changes. You fill the room with stirring sound. You're playing Bach, and you're better than ever. The audience lets you know it with their applause.

Now shift to another scene. This time you're onstage in a packed arena. You're playing with a popular rock band. The drummer pounds out a lively beat as the singers wail into the mics.

Boyd Tinsley performs with the Dave Matthews Band in a 2009 concert in San Francisco.

Sergey Ryabtsev **(left)** plays violin with the punk band Gogol Bordello in 2007.

The crowd can't get enough. When it's time for your violin solo, you don't disappoint them. The fans go wild for you.

Hey, hold on a minute. Something's wrong. A violin in a rock band?

No. You read it right. The violin is really special. It can be used in many types of music. It's also one of the most beautiful-sounding instruments ever invented. Want to know more about the violin? Keep reading. It's what this book is all about.

THE QUEEN OF INSTRUMENTS

The violin is a finely crafted instrument with a high, clear sound. Some insist that the violin sounds more like the human voice than any other instrument. When played well, the violin can bring both smiles and tears to listeners. It's been called the queen of instruments.

WE ARE FAMILY

You come from a family. You may look or sound a lot like your family members. Did anyone ever tell you that you have your brother's laugh or your mom's eyes?

Instruments are grouped in families too. The violin is in the string family. Some other string instruments are the viola, the cello, and the double bass. All these instruments have curvy wooden bodies and wooden necks. They also have four strings stretched across them. Their sound comes from the movement of their strings. The musician either plucks the strings or draws a bow across them.

String instruments look a lot alike except for their very different sizes. The violin is the smallest string instrument, while the double bass is the largest. The smaller the instrument, the higher the pitch it has.

So can you guess which string instrument has the highest pitch? Hope your answer was the violin.

This string quartet features (from left to right) a violin, a cello, a viola, and a double bass.

WHY PLAY THE VIOLIN?

There are lots of reasons to pick the violin. Here are just a few:

SIZE MATTERS

The violin is an instrument that fits most players perfectly. That's because violins come in lots of different sizes. There are violins for people of every age and build. There are even some for preschoolers. This way the youngest students learn to play on an instrument that feels just right.

The size you pick will depend on how big you are and what you feel most comfortable playing. Yet let's say you started playing when you were three. What if you keep on playing throughout your lifetime? Then you'd probably use several different sizes of violins.

The youngest violin players use the smallest sized violins.

Luckily, even a full-size violin is still a small instrument. You can put it in a case and carry it around with you. A violin can easily fit on a plane, a bus, or a train. You don't have to buy an extra seat for it. A lot of other instruments aren't so easy to cart around. You can't take a harp or a piano on the school bus with you.

A NIFTY, THRIFTY ITEM

Some instruments are very costly. If you want to buy a cello, a tuba, or a sax, be ready to spend a lot. Even a small, used piano isn't cheap. Violin prices tend to be lower. In many areas, you can get a used violin at a fair price. This puts the violin within reach of more families.

IMAGE AND PRIDE

Let's speak frankly. People look up to violin players. If you master the violin, you'll be respected and admired for it. You've done something very special.

Violin players play a classy instrument, and it shows!

Violins hang from the ceiling in a music store.

Musician and violin teacher Tamara McClellan calls the violin "the great equalizer." As she puts it, "When you play the violin, no one knows if you're good in math or science. People just see someone playing a highly respected, difficult instrument. Everyone thinks that child does well in everything. So a student struggling in math is now honored the way the best math student is. People know that violin players are special. They have a skill very few people have."

Playing the violin has still other benefits. Just think ahead. Can you see yourself applying to college? Playing the violin can be a big plus here. It looks great on a college application.

THE VIOLIN—A REALLY CLOSE LOOK

The violin is shaped like an hourglass. It has been compared to the female body. Some violin parts are named after body parts too. The violin has a neck as well as a back. It has a small waist. That's the slim middle section. The violin's belly is its front. Its sides are called ribs. Here are some other parts of the violin.

...IECE

...piece is the
...f wood to which
...om ends of the
...e attached.

BRIDGE

The bridge is the wooden piece that holds the strings in place.

FINE TUNERS

The fine tuners are metal screws on the tailpiece. They are used to make minor changes in tuning.

F-HOLES

The f-holes are openings in the violin on both sides of the bridge. They are shaped like an

...attached
...e violin. You rest
...chin rest while playing

SCROLL AND PEGS

The scroll is the fancy curled piece at the top of the violin's neck. The scroll is often hand carved. Four wooden pegs stick out of the scroll. Each of the violin's four strings is wound around a peg. The pegs are turned to tighten or loosen the strings. This is how the violin is tuned.

STRINGS

The violin has four strings. They differ in thickness. The thinner strings make high sounds. The thicker strings make low sounds.

FINGERBOARD

The fingerboard is a wooden strip attached to the violin's neck. It extends over part of the belly too. Violinists press the strings against the fingerboard to play different notes.

BOW

A violin bow is usually made of wood and horsehair. The hair comes from a horse's tail. The horsehair is stretched between two parts called the tip and the frog. A part called the tension screw can tighten the horsehair as needed.

Garage-band guitarists can really rock out. But you make a different impression when you play the violin.

What if you put down that you play guitar? Some people may picture a kid in a garage band who can barely play. Playing piano is not like playing the violin either. People often think of kids forced by their parents to take lessons year after year. But a violin player is always a star! Those fabulous fiddlers are admired.

There are more reasons to play too. You don't have to become a professional musician to benefit from it. "Learning to play the violin is great training," notes violinist Martin Goldman. "It can help you in anything you decide to do later. Playing the violin helps build character. It teaches self-discipline. It shows you that you have to work hard for success. That's a lesson worth learning."

The viola on the right looks a lot like the violin on the left. But they are two different instruments, and each has its own special sound.

MEET THE VIOLA

Try telling people you play the viola. They may think they heard you wrong. "Don't you mean the violin?" they may ask. No, you don't.

The viola is a close relative of the violin. It looks like the violin, but it's a little bigger. It also has a slightly lower, mellower sound. Does this sound like your kind of instrument? Check it out. You might become a terrific viola player!

Yet in the end, there's really only one good reason to play the violin. You have to love the sound of the instrument. You have to like the feel of it next to your body.

To quote violinist Irwin Rubin, "The violin is not like other instruments. It's not like playing the piano. The violin rests on your body. The bow is in your hand. When you play, the violin becomes part of you. With it you can make beautiful music. You can let the world know how you feel. There's nothing like it."

CHAPTER TWO

DIFFERENT STROKES FOR DIFFERENT FOLKS

You can't keep a good sound down. The violin has broken out of the orchestra pit in a big way. It's true that violins are often used in classical music (timeless, serious music including opera, chamber music, and symphony). And as a violin student, you will likely study a *lot* of classical music. That's because this music is great for putting new techniques to use and learning more advanced skills. It's also some of the most beautiful music ever written.

But violinists have branched out into other areas too. These days they play different types of music in all kinds of settings.

14

Violinists play many types of music—not just classical.

Some are true trailblazers. Could you be one of these violinists someday?

GET READY TO ROCK

What's your dream? Would you like to play rock music on your violin? Some popular rock bands are doing just that. One such band is the British group Keane. They use many instruments you wouldn't expect them to use. A piano is their lead instrument. And on some of their latest recordings, you can hear the violin and sax. The result is a one-of-a-kind indie-rock sound.

Like the idea of blending rock and classical music? Then you may be a fan of the Vitamin String Quartet. It's made up of a group of rotating Los Angeles musicians. They play the music of cutting-edge rock acts without drums or guitars. They use violins, violas, and cellos instead. Their special sound has won them lots of fans.

The British band Keane performs in Hong Kong, China, in 2009.

MEET THE DOUBLE BASS

The violin can be used to play an amazing variety of music. But what if you decide it's not for you? Maybe a larger instrument is more your style. If that's the case, you might like the double bass.

The double bass has a deep, rich tone. Its large size and unusual sound make it a standout in any orchestra.

There's just one problem with the double bass. You might have to wait until you're bigger to play it. Double basses are usually about 6 feet (2 meters) tall. That's as tall as a fairly tall man. This instrument is too big to hold like a violin. The musician usually stands or sits on a high stool to play it. The double bass is the biggest instrument in the string section of an orchestra.

Other violinists have left their mark on the world of rock as well. Maybe you like the group Yellowcard. This band plays songs that are a blend of pop and rock. What makes Yellowcard stand out from other bands that play this kind of music? Many fans think it's Sean Mackin, the band's violinist. His violin playing adds a special flavor to the music.

The hard rock Arkansas group Evanescence also likes the fresh feel the violin can bring to rock. It used the violin in the group's hit song "Whisper." Popular older groups such as U2 and R.E.M. have also used the violin in their recordings. Some people feel these groups have made it cool for kids to play the violin.

It's likely that the number of rock violin players will grow. Some schools have even started offering electric violin classes. Rock musicians often use this type of violin. Does electric violin sound like your kind of thing? Find out if electric violin classes are offered at your school or community center. Some summer music camps teach electric violin as well.

LOVIN' THAT COUNTRY MUSIC

Violins have long been used in country music. You might not have known it because country musicians call their violins fiddles. You may have thought about taking up the violin but not the fiddle. Yet there's no difference between

Some electric violins look pretty wild!

Violinist Martie Maguire performs with the Dixie Chicks in 2003.

these two instruments. The only difference is the style of music that they're used to play.

Martie Maguire of the country band the Dixie Chicks is a fiddler. Maguire began playing classical violin when she was just five. By twelve she started learning to play country-style. These lessons were a gift for her twelfth birthday.

MEET THE CELLO

What string instrument is bigger than a violin but smaller than a double bass? It's the cello!

A full-size cello is about 50 inches (127 centimeters) high. That may be just about your height. It rests on the floor when you play it. Musicians hold it between their knees to play.

Have you ever heard the velvet-smooth sound of the cello? It's enough to make you fall in love with the instrument.

As a teenager, Maguire was part of a four-girl country band. The group played at country music festivals. That was how the girls earned money in high school. Maguire later played in her college's orchestra. In 1989 she joined the Dixie Chicks. The rest is country music history.

Like your violin music lively and quick? Country or bluegrass violin may be for you. Many areas have jam sessions. Fiddlers play at these. Sometimes the public can listen for free. Maybe your parents could take you to one. See if there are any country music festivals in your area as well. The more you listen, the more you'll learn about this style of music.

ALL THAT JAZZ

Violinists also play jazz. Jazz violin is not as formal as classical violin. It tends not to be as lively as country fiddling either. Jazz violin players have less structure to their music. They sometimes make up part of what they play while they're playing. This is known as improvisation. It lets jazz musicians develop their own ideas musically. Yet they still play with the other members of their band.

Jazz violinist Nicole Yarling compares improvisation to writing a story. "When you write a story," she says, "you take words and put them into sentences. You put the sentences into paragraphs. The paragraphs make up the story. It's sort of the same way with jazz. You learn the language of jazz by listening. Then you take that language and put it together to make your own music."

FROM BACH TO POP

Escala (above) is a string quartet made up of four very talented young women. At first glance, you might think they played classical music. But you'd be wrong. These ladies rock!

Two of them are violinists. They were trained to play classical music. Then they switched to pop. They proved to be great at both kinds of music. It just shows that a good violinist can do just about anything.

TALENTED TEEN JAZZ GUY

Jonathan Russell is a jazz violinist. This talented teen started taking violin lessons when he was three. By the time he was five, he'd begun playing jazz.

Jonathan Russell

Jonathan has played at jazz festivals across the United States. He's wowed audiences in Europe too. At nine years old, he'd already won awards. At ten Jonathan became the youngest jazz violin player ever invited to take part in a master class at the Lincoln Center for the Performing Arts in New York. Master classes are taught by well-known and highly respected musicians.

Some people think that young jazz players like Jonathan Russell can be especially important to violin music. Their music may connect young people to an older generation of violin lovers. Could you join the ranks of jazz violinists someday? That might be a great choice. Start listening to lots of jazz violin music. That will help you decide if this style should be your style.

CHAPTER THREE

YOU AND THE VIOLIN:
PERFECT TOGETHER?

You love music and want it to be a big part of your life. You've decided to learn to play an instrument, and you've picked the violin. Did you make the right choice? There is no simple answer to that question. Different people choose the violin for different reasons.

Sometimes there isn't much of a choice. Often kids start playing through the band program at their school. Not every instrument is offered. Yet you just might get the right instrument for you. That's how it was for violinist Janice Muller.

Many people pick up an instrument because a family member plays it.

Have you ever heard of David Garrett? He's the world's fastest violinist. He became a YouTube sensation by playing the song "Flight of the Bumblebee" in 1 minute 6.56 seconds. That guy's got really fast fingers! Keep practicing. You'll pick up speed too.

"I started playing when I was about ten years old," she said. "There weren't a lot of choices available for kids where we lived. You were limited to whatever instruments your school offered. At my school, string instruments were brought in. You could pick either the viola or the violin. I picked the violin. I really liked its sound. It was a great choice for me."

In other cases, you might pick an instrument because of something in your background. Maybe your mom or dad plays violin CDs all the time. You've heard that music since you were a baby. Now you want to play it yourself.

Other young people have picked the violin because their brother or sister plays it. Often they end up doing duets with their sibling. In some cases, whole families are violin players. The parents play too.

WORDS OF WISDOM

What does it take to be a good violinist? Consider these words of wisdom from violinist Tamara McClellan. "A good violinist pays attention to details. The pitch has to be exact. The rhythm must be precise too. The music has to tell a story. No one wants to hear out-of-tune music or careless rhythms. Every note counts or it wouldn't be there."

For still other people, the violin just seemed to end up in their lives. That's how violinist Irwin Rubin started. "My grandmother bought a violin from my uncle," he explained. "She gave it to me. That's how I wound up with the violin. I had it at home, so (I started taking) lessons. Years later, I came to really love the violin. That's when I thanked my parents for making me practice."

Often people come to play the violin by chance. Violinist Dmitri Pogorelov has an interesting story about how he came to play the violin. "One day," he said, "when I was still very little, I asked my parents to buy me a toy. My parents, who were both professional musicians, brought home something for me that night. It was a child-size violin. By then it was already too late to explain to them that was not what I had in mind. So I began learning to play the violin."

Yet many young people who start to learn the violin don't stick with it. The violin is not an easy instrument to play. When you play the violin, your

IT TAKES WORK

Violinist Martin Goldman says that a willingness to practice and follow through on things is essential to anyone who wants to play the violin. You can't learn to play well overnight. As Goldman puts it, "A young person has to be willing to do what it takes [to play the violin], and it takes work."

right and left hands are doing two completely different things at the same time. You press down on the strings with the fingertips of your left hand. Your right hand holds the bow as you draw it across the strings. You also have to learn to tell if you're playing the right notes. There's a lot going on at once. And it's up to you to make it all happen smoothly.

Learning to play the violin takes a lot of time and effort. So what makes some people go on while others give up? Many violinists believe that you have to really love the violin's sound. Some say if you love the sound, you'll love the instrument. Kids who feel this way often want to practice.

Playing the violin takes coordination. Each hand is doing something different. You also need to watch the music.

The violin is like a best friend to them. They want to spend a lot of time with it.

Violinist Thomas D. Moore explained what it was like for him:

When I was a child, my mother started me on piano lessons. But when I was in fourth grade, the music program at my school began. I came home and told my mother that I wanted to play the violin. She laughed and said I was having a hard enough time with the piano. She . . . reminded me that the violin is a lot harder than the piano.

But I begged and I pleaded, and finally my parents gave in. They rented some horrible violin from a music store for two weeks. The violin is difficult to play, but if it's a bad instrument, it's even harder on the child. You can't make a beautiful sound on a bad instrument. It's really frustrating.

I took that violin to school and played it there too. After about six days, my music teacher called my parents. He said that I had talent and that they needed to get me a decent instrument. When they finally got a good violin for me, I took it up to my room. I began playing it and wouldn't come down for dinner that night. I played for four hours. When I finally came down, I could play four pieces.

CHAPTER FOUR

WHAT DOES IT TAKE TO PLAY THE VIOLIN?

Have you ever heard this joke? A tourist in New York City needs directions. He asks a passerby how to get to Carnegie Hall. The passerby answers, "Practice, practice, practice."

Although this is a joke, it's no joke that musicians need to practice. Practice is important for anyone who plays the violin.

The Cross Border Orchestra of Ireland performs to a sold-out audience at Carnegie Hall in New York in 2005.

PRACTICE MAKES PERFECT

Practice is especially important for beginners. New violinists have many new skills to learn. Violinist Marcia Littley de Arias puts it this way: "New violin students go through some tough times. It's not like playing the piano. A piano student can play something that sounds lovely fairly soon. It's harder with the violin. You have to train your mind, your fingers, and your ears. You really have to work at it. It can take a long time. Violin players have to have patience."

HEY, LET'S PLAY THE LATIN WAY

QUESTION: What string instrument is often played in the Andes Mountains of Bolivia and Peru?

ANSWER: It's a nifty little number called the charango! Charangos are small enough to easily carry and fun to play. They were once made from the shells of armadillos. That was really bad news for the animal. These days the charango is made of wood. It is a widely played and much-loved folk instrument.

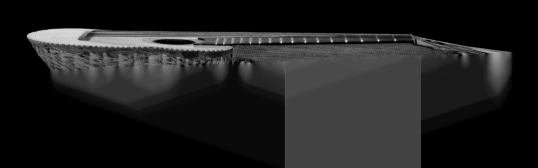

Practice time might mean playing alone, or it might mean playing with an orchestra or band.

How much should you practice? A half hour to forty-five minutes a day will usually do for a beginner. As you become more skilled, you can increase your practice time. The more you practice, the better you'll get.

Practice lets you develop the technique and skills you need. It also helps these skills blend together. After a while, the music just seems to flow out of you and your instrument. You'll find that your mind and hands have become partners with your violin.

Violinist Thomas D. Moore explains how this happens. "If you practice enough," he says, "you develop muscle memory. This can rescue you if you slip up during a performance. If you don't know where you are, your fingers take over. It happens without you even thinking about it."

DO YOU NEED A PRACTICE PLAN?

Many music teachers want their students to have a practice plan. The idea behind a plan is to keep you on track. You define your goals and stick to your plan. That should help to get you where you want to go musically.

Part of your plan should be about how often you practice the violin. As little as twenty minutes of practice can bring about results if it's done every day. It's better to do this than to practice one day a week for four hours.

Being focused should also be part of your practice plan. Think about what you're doing each time you pick up your violin. Don't let your mind wander. During practice you shouldn't be thinking about a movie you saw or the pizza you want to order. One violin teacher gave his students this motto to follow: "If your mind leaves the room, take your body with it."

Violinist Tamara McClellan describes good practice habits this way: "It's not how many hours you put into your instrument that matters. It's how you use those hours that counts."

She adds, "A person needs to practice wisely. Don't spend most of your time practicing what you already know. Practice what you don't know. Then put it all together. Practice regularly and when you're not tired. Quality practicing goes a long way."

PUERTO RICAN STRINGS

The Scots have the bagpipes. The Irish have the harp. The Puerto Ricans have the cuatro.

The cuatro is a guitarlike instrument. It's shaped like a violin but is a little more rounded. Can you count in Spanish? If so, you know that the word cuatro means "four." In early times, the cuatro had four strings. Modern cuatros have five sets of double strings.

The cuatro is often played at gatherings and festivals. It's Puerto Rico's national instrument.

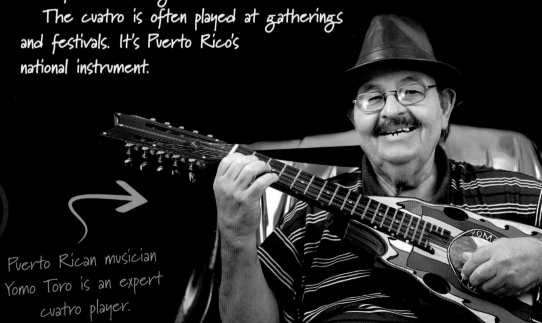

Puerto Rican musician Yomo Toro is an expert cuatro player.

An experienced violin player can handle almost any problem during a performance.

SURVIVING ONSTAGE

You've practiced for months. You've really tried hard. Your big day is here. You have a solo in a violin recital.

You're very excited. But that's not all you feel. You're also scared. You've wanted to be onstage all year. Now you wish you could hide in a cave somewhere.

Lots of people get nervous before a performance. The best cure for stage fright is to be prepared. Also know your weak areas. Work on these before the recital date. Violinist

Thomas D. Moore explains, "The quality and amount of your preparation make all the difference. You have to know that you know it. Then you're less apt to be nervous."

But what if you really know your material? Things can still go wrong at performances. You can have a memory slip. The strings on your violin can break.

Outdoor performances can be especially troublesome. In one case, a strong wind blew a violinist's music all over the lawn. Another time a violinist was asked to play in front of a fountain. The fountain was unexpectedly turned on. The violinist and her music were soaked.

AN "OH, NO!" VIOLIN PERFORMANCE

Joseph Merlin of Huy, Belgium, invented roller skates. He was also a violin player. Merlin decided to use his violin to introduce roller skates to the world. In about 1760, he roller-skated into a crowded ballroom while playing his violin. But things didn't go as well as he had hoped. Merlin hadn't yet figured out how to stop on skates. He crashed into a full-length mirror. The worst part was that he broke his lovely violin.

What do you do when these things happen? The answer is as old as show business itself. You smile and do your best to go on. Remember that sooner or later, these things happen to everyone. It doesn't make you any less of a musician. Besides, audiences tend to be very forgiving when they are listening to good music.

SUCCESS!

If you learn to play the violin, be proud of yourself. It will mean you've mastered the queen of instruments. You can delight and entertain audiences. And the violin will repay you for all the time and work you put into learning to play it. It will bring the joy of beautiful music to you and those who hear you for years to come.

QUIZ: IS THE VIOLIN RIGHT FOR YOU?

Which of these statements describes you best? Please record your answers on a separate sheet of paper.

1. **If at first you don't succeed,**
    - **A.** You try, try again. You like to finish what you start. People say you're the determined type.
    - **B.** You feel that a lack of success means it wasn't meant to be. You prefer to try something else you may be better at.

2. **When you hear a good piece of music,**
    - **A.** You get really into all the sounds. You feel as if you could listen to the piece forever!
    - **B.** You think it sounds good, but you don't usually get too absorbed in it. You'd rather spend time working on art or learning new soccer moves than listening closely to music.

3. **When you're doing a task that requires fine motor skills,**
    - **A.** Your fingers are quick and nimble. Detailed tasks are fun for you.
    - **B.** You tend to drop things or get frustrated. Taking bike rides or playing video games is more up your alley than working with your hands.

4. **When you picture yourself playing an instrument in your school band,**
    - **A.** You imagine yourself playing something small. You think petite can be neat! The tuba is not for you.
    - **B.** You imagine yourself playing the bass drum, the cello . . . anything big! You love the sound and feel of a large musical instrument.

5. **When you think about practicing your instrument,**
    - **A.** You get really excited. You think studying an instrument sounds like fun!
    - **B.** You like music, but you can think of other things you'd rather do. Giving up free time to practice every day doesn't sound worth it.

Were your answers mostly A's?

If so, the violin may just be the right choice for you!

GLOSSARY

bluegrass: a form of U.S. country music

bow: a wooden rod with horsehairs stretched from end to end. Bows are used to play the violin and some other string instruments.

duet: a musical performance in which two performers play together

fiddle: a violin that is used to play country music

improvisation: making up parts of the music you play while you are playing it

jam session: a get-together where musicians meet to play their instruments

jazz: a form of music characterized by loose structure and improvisation

pitch: the highness or lowness of a sound

solo: a musical performance in which a performer plays alone

string family: a group of instruments that produce sound through the movement of their strings

SOURCE NOTES

9   Tamara McClellan, e-mail to author, June 6, 2009.

12   Martin Goldman, interview with author, May 30, 2009.

13   Irwin Rubin, telephone conversation with author, June 4, 2009.

19–20   Nicole Yarling, telephone conversation with author, June 24, 2009.

23   Janice Muller, interview with author, June 7, 2009.

24   McClellan.

24   Rubin.

25   Dmitri Pogorelov, e-mail to author, June 20, 2009.

25   Goldman.

27   Thomas D. Moore, interview with author, May 31, 2009.

29   Marcia Littley de Arias, interview with author, June 23, 2009.

30   Moore.

31   Littley.

31–32   McClellan.

34   Moore.

SELECTED BIBLIOGRAPHY

Courvoisier, Karl. *The Technique of Violin Playing: The Joachim Method*. Mineola, NY: Dover Publications, 2008.

Kempter, Susan. *How Muscles Learn: Teaching Violin with the Body in Mind*. Van Nuys, CA: Alfred Publishing Co., 2003.

Martens, Frederick. *Violin Mastery: Interviews with Heifetz, Auer, Kreisler, and Others*. Mineola, NY: Dover Publications, 2006.

McCabe, Larry. *How to Play Fiddle: Beginner Book and CD*. Danvers, MA: Santorella Publications, 2005.

Rush, Mark. *Playing the Violin: An Illustrated Guide*. New York: Routledge, 2006.

FOR MORE INFORMATION

Dallas Symphony Orchestra: Kids
http://www.dsokids.com
Visit this website to learn about the violin and listen to the sounds it makes. Don't miss the link to fun music-related games!

Franks, Katie. *I Want to Be a Rock Star*. New York: PowerKids Press, 2007. This book offers an exciting look at the career of a rock star. Meeting fans, playing concerts, going on tour, and more are covered.

Josephson, Judith Pinkerton. *Bold Composer: A Story about Ludwig van Beethoven*. Minneapolis: Millbrook Press, 2007. Josephson tells the engaging life story of Beethoven, one of the world's best-loved composers.

Kenney, Karen Latchana. *Cool Rock Music: Create & Appreciate What Makes Music Great!* Edina, MN: Abdo, 2008. This book introduces rock music and the instruments used to play it. There's also information on writing a rock song and making a rock video.

Violin Care and Maintenance
http://www.centrum.is/hansi/maintenance.html
Check out this website for some great information on how to best care for your violin.

THE VIOLINISTS WHO HELPED WITH THIS BOOK

This book could not have been written without the help of these violinists. All provided great insights into what it is like to love and play the violin.

MARCIA LITTLEY DE ARIAS

Marcia Littley de Arias, a Juilliard graduate, is a founding member of the Amernet String Quartet. She's won many awards including grand prize at the Fischoff National Chamber Music Competition.

MARTIN GOLDMAN

Martin Goldman received music degrees from the Manhattan School of Music and Yale University. He's performed with orchestras and opera houses in Brussels, Belgium; and Florence and Rome, Italy.

TAMARA MCCLELLAN

Tamara McClellan is an accomplished violinist as well as an elementary school music teacher.

THOMAS D. MOORE

Thomas D. Moore has held positions with chamber and symphony orchestras. He was formerly a concertmaster for the Florida Philharmonic and is a professor of violin and chamber music at the New World School of the Arts.

JANICE MULLER

Janice Muller is a classical violinist based in Miami, Florida. She is known for her work as a soloist.

DMITRI POGORELOV

Dmitri Pogorelov is a prize-winning violinist and respected performer. He won first prize in both the 2005 National Society of Arts and Letters Violin Competition and the 2004 William C. Byrd International Young Artist Competition for Strings.

IRWIN RUBIN

Violinist Irwin Rubin has a repertoire of some of the greatest songs ever written. He has years of experience playing in musical productions and at special events.

NICOLE YARLING

Nicole Yarling has a master's degree in music education from Columbia University. She's been part of South Florida's musical world as a violinist working in jazz, rock, rhythm and blues, and experimental music.

INDEX

PHOTO ACKNOWLEDGMENTS

The images in this book are used with the permission of: © iStockphoto.com/Chris Hutchison, pp. 1, 2, 3 (left), 10-11, all page backgrounds; © iStockphoto.com/Arpad Nagy-Bagoly, pp. 1 and all page backgrounds; © Douglas Mason/Getty Images, p. 4; © Michael Burnell/Redferns/Getty Images, p. 5; © Dorling Kindersley/Getty Images, pp. 6, 29; © Toshi Kawano/Taxi Japan/Getty Images, p. 7; © iStockphoto.com/Evgeniy Gorbunov, p. 8; © Grant Faint/Photodisc/Getty Images, p. 9; © Rgbspace/Dreamstime.com, p. 12; © Laura Frenkel/Dreamstime.com, p. 13; © Gregory Costanzo/Stone/Getty Images, pp. 14-15; © Tungstar/Getty Images, p. 15; © Roma Koshel/Dreamstime.com, p. 16; © Image Source/Getty Images, p. 17; © Max Franklin/Getty Images, p. 18; © Dave Hogan/Getty Images, p. 20; © Lezlie Sterling/Sacramento Bee/ZUMA Press, p. 21; © Dorgie Productions/Photographer's Choice/Getty Images, p. 22; AP Photo/Axel Heimken, Pool, p. 23; © Thatcher Keats/Photonica/Getty Images, p. 24; © Nicholas Sutcliffe/Dreamstime.com, p. 25; © age fotostock/SuperStock, pp. 26, 32; © Paul McErlane/Alamy, p. 28; © Robert Van Der Hilst/Reportage/Getty Images, p. 30; © JGI/Blend Images/Getty Images, p. 31; © iStockphoto.com/Yenwen Lu, p. 33; © Mike Kemp/Rubberball Productions/Getty Images, p. 34.

Front cover: © iStockphoto.com/Chris Hutchison (violins); © iStockphoto.com/Arpad Nagy-Bagoly (sheet music).